THE THUNDERBIRD POEMS

ALSO BY ARMAND GARNET RUFFO

Poetry

Opening in the Sky
Grey Owl: The Mystery of Archie Belaney
At Geronimo's Grave

Non-fiction

Norval Morrisseau: Man Changing into Thunderbird

Film

A Windigo Tale

Editor

(Ad)dressing Our Words: Aboriginal Perspectives on Aboriginal Literatures
An Anthology of Canadian Native Literature in English

THE
THUNDERBIRD
POEMS

Armand Garnet Ruffo

HARBOUR
PUBLISHING

1 2 3 4 5 — 19 18 17 16 15

Harbour Publishing Co. Ltd.
P.O. Box 219, Madeira Park, BC, V0N 2H0
www.harbourpublishing.com

Edited by Daniel David Moses and Rebecca Hendry
Cover design by Anna Comfort O'Keeffe
Text design by Mary White
Printed and bound in Canada

Harbour Publishing acknowledges the support of the Canada Council for the Arts, which last year invested $157 million to bring the arts to Canadians throughout the country. We also gratefully acknowledge financial support from the Government of Canada through the Canada Book Fund and from the Province of British Columbia through the BC Arts Council and the Book Publishing Tax Credit.

Cataloguing data available from Library and Archives Canada
ISBN 978-1-55017-706-0 (paper)
ISBN 978-1-55017-707-7 (ebook)

In memory of Norval Morrisseau
and for Victoria Cuthbert and Linda Jordan

"My aim is to reassemble the pieces of a once proud culture and to show the dignity and bravery of my people, the Great Ojibway."

—NORVAL MORRISSEAU

Table of Contents

MOTHER OF ALL THINGS

INDIAN CANOE

In the course of writing *Man Changing into Thunderbird*, a book about the life of Norval Morrisseau, I found that Morrisseau's art moved me in such a manner that a natural and spontaneous response to it was to write poetry. From the beginning, my goal was not to replicate the paintings in the poems, although a couple of the pieces come close; rather, I wanted to concentrate on tying the paintings to events in Morrisseau's life and, accordingly, to the artist's sources of inspiration, including Ojibway epistemology. And although the poems themselves move in chronological order through the paintings, from his earliest to his latter work, they reference events across time. By way of explanation, I will say that throughout the process of writing, I strived to let the paintings themselves determine the content of the poetry, wherever that might take me. Initially, I thought I would write a few ekphrastic poems based on the paintings I admired most, and which it seemed to me gave insight into the artist. However, as I learned more about Morrisseau's life and immersed myself in the paintings, more poems appeared. My plan was to include all the poems in the one book, but as the poems increased I realized there were too many to include them all. I also realized that I had a complete book of poetry. *The Thunderbird Poems* includes all the poems I wrote during this period of contemplation on the art and life of Norval Morrisseau.

—Armand Garnet Ruffo

LIFE SCROLL

The sacred birch bark scrolls of the Ojibway were created by visionary shamans and hold the knowledge of a people steeped in a world of Manitous (Manidoog), or "Demi-gods"—as Norval Morrisseau referred to them in English. The scrolls are among the artist's most important influences.

⊕

Life Scroll, n.d.

Where your dreams find you in the blue lake of your mind
and vibrate to the surface like a speckled trout.

Where a long-forgotten rock face turns into your face
and vision points in the direction of youth, middle age, old age.

Where gnarled fingers slide with precision along a map of birch bark
and belief and ritual hold hands.

Where there is no one but you and the echoes of ancestors
in the halls of your loneliest night.

Where all creation rests on the back of the strongest and depends
upon the grasp of the weakest, and all is related.

Where you learn the art of listening and the old words drip
into the stone bowl of your deafness.

Where you learn the art of seeing and the old signs are owl eyes
that stare into the forest of your ignorance.

Where you must learn how to love and be loved
and admit that your journey too will soon come to an end.

*Images of Mishipashoo (or Mishipesheu) can be found among the pictographs
scattered throughout Ojibway country. In the early 1960s, Selwyn Dewdney,
an artist and part-time anthropologist working for the Royal Ontario Museum,
gave Norval Morrisseau access to his manuscript* Indian Rock Paintings of the
Great Lakes.

⊕

The Mishipashoo, 1958–60

You are asleep when they come.
In a cage of dream
you cannot wake from.
On a stretch of beach
they crawl out of the water.
Surround you. Move in.

Heavy heads and spiked tails
sway like trees. Crunch
of bone in their sharp mouths.
You run under pale stars
under the bloodshot eye of the moon
as they come slithering toward you.

Suddenly the ground begins to tremble.
In front of you is a giant white buffalo.
You plead for help.
The sky turns brilliant blue
as he shakes his ghostly head
and says it is all about belief.

You look back and the Mishipashoos are gone.
You are in the presence of power.
In the buffalo's mouth
is a scarf cut from a piece of sky.
He instructs you to take it.
Blue, the colour of protection.

The perspective of this painting differs from all of Norval Morrisseau's other work.
He places the viewer in the midst of the shaking tent ceremony. We seem to be
floating above the scene as though we are dreaming it or someone inside the tent is
dreaming us.

⊕

Ancestors Performing the Ritual of the Shaking Tent, c. 1958–61

You are standing outside the ceremony
gazing upon three red-hooded members of the secret
Midewewin Medicine Society
in the midst of the mysterious
and powerful Jeeskum,
the shaking tent ceremony.

Of the two standing figures,
one is drumming,
the second is shaking a rattle,
the third figure whose back is toward you
is sitting, presumably praying. Centred
in the background a wigwam stitched together
from hide or bark.
Staked to the ground.

The fourth figure you do not see.
The Conjurer is inside the tent.
The blessed Shaman.
The one who makes things tremble.
The one who provides the questions.
The one sanctioned by gift.

Bound hand and foot,
he first calls in Mikkinnuk, Turtle,
to interpret for all the other spirits.
Mikkinnuk is no ordinary turtle,
but a spirit
embodied in the shell of a turtle.

After the appropriate ritual,
the prayers and songs
of praise and humility,
if the spirits approve,
if the ceremony is strong enough,
Mikkinnuk will enter the tent
and blow away the Shaman's bindings.

Then whoever or whatever may be… follows,
the spirits exuding such power
that each response they give
lifts the tent off the ground,
wants to tear it from its mooring.
A cacophony of voices slamming into it,
all the force of a storm.
In another time and place,
it is Morrisseau inside the tent.

"So long as I have my visions and they are truly mine then my paintings will also be truly mine." Norval Morrisseau spoke of his vision quest in vivid detail. He loved his grandfather dearly and credited him for everything that he knew about the customs and lore of his people.

⊕

Sacred Bear from Vision, 1959–60

Norval is twelve when his grandfather Potan Nanakonagos takes him for his vision quest. It is the time for the youth to leave childhood behind and move to the next stage of his seven cycles of life. That summer they paddle to an island not far from Sand Point. When they arrive, the first thing they do is make a scaffold out of the few birch trees nearby. Potan chops them down with his axe and fashions them into poles, lashing them together with braids of moose hide. Norval will spend four nights with no food and as little water as possible, suspended twenty feet in the air.

Potan tells the boy that during this time a guiding spirit will come and take pity on him. This spirit will guide him for the rest of his life. But beware, his grandfather warns, when it comes, make sure not to open your eyes. If you are fortunate it will come at night when you cannot see it. It may take any shape, a thundercloud, a breeze, an eagle, an otter, anything. Norval is scared, but his absolute faith and love for his grandfather gives him courage. Seeing the boy's fear, Potan assures him he will not be too far away.

During the day Norval lies on the scaffold overlooking the great expanse of Lake Nipigon, white-tipped waves in all directions. And on the opposite shore, the impenetrable green lushness of the bush making him feel more alone than ever. As he watches, he tries not to think of his hunger rolling through his stomach and tightening it like a drum. To ease the ache, he wets his lips but does not swallow the water. Instead he sends it over the side, to the ground below.

At night, raised among the stars, cloud drifting across the pale moon, every sound seems to claw its way toward him. The trees alongside creaking in the breeze. The flutter of wings in the branches. The scamper of feet in the brush below. His whole body wound up to the point of snapping, he must force himself not to scramble down from his perch and flee. Exposed, vulnerable, as though set on a platter for the taking, he burrows himself in the blanket his grandmother gave him and focuses on the light of his grandfather's fire on the shore across the narrows. Then, exhausted from worry and fatigue, he closes his eyes and waits.

On the third night it comes.

By this time, having drifted in and out of consciousness all day, he is uncertain of whether he is asleep or awake when he hears it. Unlike all the sounds he has heard before, this he knows is different, and it makes him go absolutely still, sucking in what air he can and holding his breath. From down in the darkness below comes what he will later describe as a thumping sound moving across the ground, getting closer and closer.

Finally, it is near him, moving around at the bottom of the scaffold. And then, in an instant, a guttural sniffing at the end of his feet, the feel of warm breath through the blanket, moving up his legs to his hips, arms, shoulders… and try as he might, Norval cannot hold back any longer. Despite his grandfather's warning, he opens his eyes.

And there before him is a huge bear. A gasp, and Norval is up and scrambling. Blood pounding through him, he musters what little strength he has left and climbs down the scaffold. Running to the shore, he yells for his grandfather to help him. Potan, who has been patiently waiting for something to happen, calls back to him that he will be right there. It is only upon hearing his grandfather's canoe approaching that Norval turns back to the scaffold and realizes the height of it. And wonders how such a bear could have stood next to him and, in the opening of his eyes, disappeared.

Stepping out of his canoe, the first thing his grandfather wants to know is whether or not Norval looked. Ashamed, the boy admits that he did. The old man shakes his head slowly, emphasizing he told him not to look, but he does not shame the boy. Instead he tells him a story.

> Everything depended upon Bear.
> It was he who was to bring
> the message of everlasting life

20

to the people. But the weight
he carried from the Creator was very heavy
and Bear had to struggle.
Three times he tried
to break through
from the spirit world
to the world of the people
and failed.
On the fourth try he stuck out his tongue
and like an arrow
he passed through
to the other side.

With a grin, he also tells Norval that Bear is so powerful he owns three cities. They could be Chicago, Montreal and New York. He is one of the richest bears in the world. You could have had all the success you want. Yet, despite looking, still you will have a little. All the same, he took pity on you. He came to visit you.

Norval will always remember these words from his grandfather. And he will spend countless hours rendering his vision of Bear. The Shaman Protected by Bear Power, Sacred Bear Quest, The Medicine Bear, Sacred Bear from Vision—all these and more he will paint. Many years later, Norval, with his own grin, will say: If I had not looked, I could have had much further success than what I have now, but I am not doing too badly. This is what, my people, I would like them to know.

Before becoming a full-time artist, Norval Morrisseau worked in the gold mines of Red Lake in remote northwestern Ontario as a flotation operator, watching over and adjusting a large vat of molten gold and chemicals. He would bring home rough filter paper to paint on.

⊕

Untitled (Thunderbird), 1960

liquid gold

life spark

the boiling mass throws its brilliance into his goggled face
— witness — to fathomless beauty — all the cruelty of the world —
he marvels at the spectacle torn from the dark earth — a crucible
of blinding light held like a story of beginning without end

on his way home the October night strokes his fevered body
like a lover as his smallness evaporates into the bush —
and up to a billion galaxies — it is then it happens —
the furious sky opens in a slit of razor daylight

the next day he leaves with a roll of mill paper under his arm
— his determination the blue fire of the smelting furnace —
and with some cheap colour from the local craft store —
he paints to understand all he has seen and heard and felt

What is the nature of power? He asks — as the kitchen table melts
in the heat of something never before witnessed — as he travels
to a place he knows instinctively — a portent signaling return —
an omen of things to come — later sold to a local trucker
for a few dollars

This early painting features a strange, terrifying creature with dead eyes. Lines of power radiate from its body. It raises the question: was it inspired by the ancient rock art of his people, or conjured out of Morrisseau's own dreams and nightmares?

⊕

Death the Devourer of Human Flesh, c.1964

Look at its ready teeth.
Its dripping tongue.
Its eyes.
Its claws.
Its horns.
Its hackles.
Its tail.

Lines of primordial power radiating like hunger.

Look inside
the white chamber
of its stomach

It's coming and there is nothing you can do about it.

No balance
in this one.
No sign
of spirit.
Nothing
but emptiness.

There are many old stories that tell of the battle between these two Manitous. It is an eternal struggle that articulates the concept of balance, for one cannot exist without the other. Norval Morrisseau is drinking heavily at the time of executing this painting, and we can see his own struggles exemplified in it.

⊕

Thunderbird and Snake, 1966

A man rides on the wings of a thunderbird.

The man's body far below is hunger he is always hunger.

For the sweet flesh of the vine.

The man prays for repentance. It does no good.

When the sun is down he goes out of his mind with appetite.

He slides along the ground. Into anything.

And dreams for his thunderbird spirit to come in for the kill.

The man wants to destroy this body that has a mind of its own.

He begins with three dots of yellow for eyes: thunderbird. man. snake.

Begins with Creation: skyworld. world. underworld.

In Norval Morrisseau's paintings, it is common to see the natural world in a state of grace. The artist presents birds, fish and animals such as bear and moose alongside human beings or even connected to them. Likewise, you often see a benevolent "Mother Earth" in radiant splendor. This painting is a startling exception.

⊕

Earth Mother, 1966

He's still using muted earth tones:
brown, green, beige, a little red.
Unlike the work from his later technicolour period,
this one comes right out of the land,
as though he's taken a hunting knife
and slit himself open,
and when it's finished it frightens him.

Put your ear to the canvas, and you will hear the rising water.

What you see is a canoe afloat with passengers.
Nanaboozho – or maybe the artist trying to save himself –
a moose, a beaver, a bird, an otter
and, of course, a tiny muskrat,
who does what the others cannot
and dives to the bottom of the great lake
and brings up a tiny morsel of soil
the Creator uses to remake the world.

All these characters, because they are characters
in the grand scheme of the story,
however, pale to the thing they are floating on:
a monstrous fanged creature,
razor teeth, serpent eyes, forked tongue,
hackles, claws, fins, a hungry belly
stuffed with human flesh and spirit.

Is this the Mother Earth we dare trample on?

Birds are a central motif in Norval Morrisseau's paintings, in which humans are often seen in the process of changing into birds, moving toward a high plane of existence. While in jail in Kenora for disturbing the peace, Morrisseau entered a province-wide prison art contest and won first place with a painting of loons.

⊕

Four Loons, 1968

LOOOOOOnLoooooooOOnnnnnLoonLOoooNLOONLOONN

M A A N G MaaangMaAAnnGGm M A A NGMaang

LOONLo o o o OOoNLoOnLoooooononononononoLOoN

M a a n g MAang m a a n g g MAAAAAAgMaanggg

Beginning in the 1960s, Norval Morrisseau did numerous self-portraits. Despite problems, such as poverty and alcoholism, he often represents himself as having shamanic power and partially transformed into a thunderbird Manitou.

⊕

Self Portrait, 1968

That's when you enter the room
and scare us with your kind of mad genius.
We can see you've been drinking again
to take the edge off, you say.
And from the look of your hands
decorated in yellow and blue and red paint,
you've been hard at work again
breaking every rule.

And with a flourish, another masterpiece
from the maestro, like a rabbit out of a hat,
as we stare in awe, half believing.
You make it look so simple.
But is it? The question falls flat
as the image you profile
in your own likeness.

All the power of the world wrapped
around you in a sleeping thunderbird
that rides your body like a second skin,
like second sight.
Do you see something we don't
with those x-ray eyes of yours?
There you go again flapping your wings
nearly levitating off the ground
as you try to explain.

This rare painting, out of the thousands credited to the artist, is one of the few to have an overt political theme or message. It becomes more profound when we learn that as a child the artist suffered sexual abuse while attending St. Joseph's Residential School in Fort William (now Thunder Bay).

⊕

White Man's Curse, 1969

Pockmarked bodies.
A pattern of dots for disease. Plague.
One brown hand leading the other.
Green for brain. Red for heart.
A missionary on a mission.
Doctrine of the crucifix.
After assimilation.
Conversion.
Who leads who?

Sweating like a beer bottle
He examines the painting.
Evil. Curse. Death.
Struggle. Struggle. Struggle.
The feel of groping flesh still suffocates him.
St. Joseph's Residential School branded.
† †
No No No No No No No No No No No No
Better to think Serenity
Bird Bear Fish
Unity.

Norval Morrisseau's grandfather Potan Nanakonagos told him many stories that connect the world of animals to the world of humans. Morrisseau's work speaks of this relationship, and about our interdependence with all living creatures.

⊕

Sacred Beaver, 1969

He learns that nothing is ever what he thinks it is.
The surface of things reflected in a lake.

He sees Ahmik, beaver, hauling a branch
Busy at work preparing for winter.

He sees a rock painting as he paddles past.
For him there is nothing between the two.

Then he is in his grandfather's voice
Who is sharing a story with him

About long ago when giant beaver roamed
The Lake Nipigon area of Great Turtle Island.

One day a thunderbird grabbed Ahmik
And lifted the squirming creature up into the sky.

And struggle as it might the beaver could not escape
Thunderbird's bloodstained hooks.

The more it sought to free itself the more
Its gashes opened and bled upon the earth below.

So that all the red ochre we see today
Used by shaman-artists of old

It is all really beaver blood.
All really about here.

About who he is, and where he comes from,
Plunged into him like a stake.

Among the Ojibway there is a form of "bad medicine," or Jeemshikiiki, called
"bear walking." In this ceremony a shaman or his apprentice turns into a bear with
the purpose of doing harm. Norval Morrisseau often spoke of his shamanic power
and implied that he too had the power to transform into a bear.

⊕

Untitled (transformation subject, shaman to bear), n.d.

He's up in Red Lake drinking in the Snakepit,
when he tells them that his people
knew things they could never fathom
– Enaadziin, he says, ways of being –
and they laugh in his face.
And the first thought that goes through his head
is to tell them to go to hell. Instead
he goes home and paints. Paints the feeling
out of himself. The side of him they don't dare see.
The thing that percolates out of him
like black coffee, rises up through his skin,
drips out of his eyes,
and spills onto the canvas. Bear Walk.
That's what the painting becomes.
A shaman with thick bear ears
and a blunt bear snout
blowing his bear breath into a new born
wrapped like a present,
an apprentice who will grow up on all fours,
growling. Who will arrive at their door
when they least expect it,
when they are snug in their bed,
one arm around a wife,
the other already around him.

SHAMAN RIDER

This painting is one of Norval Morrisseau masterpieces, picturing the artist himself on the back of the roaring thunderbird. A believer in spirit or soul travel through deep dreaming, the artist spoke of his travels through the "astral planes," adopting the language of the new-age "religion" Eckankar.

⊕

Shaman Rider, 1972

high
Morrisseau is riding   astride his beloved THUNDERBIRD
            each swoop of Massive Wings
nearly knocking him off his throne

                                    gazes
                                            down
through silver cloud to the   small earthlings
                                            below

PORTRAIT OF A SHAMAN RIDER

long flowing hair
tied back in a band of leather
jade and ruby necklace
squawking birds blown asunder
or perched royally
                observant   attentive

bound to the gift of SPIRIT   Starry Milky Way
path   of death
beacon of life
sliding through multi-layered   worlds   universes
watching new galaxies explode
                        unfold
before his eyes in radiant   living   c o l o u r
                    Descending
                            to EARTH
he never knows where he'll be
                    back
in his little tarpaper shack

in the bush
in Beardmore, waking up in Thunder Bay
at the Sea-Vue Motel   hungover   all his paintings   Gone

Or maybe he's in Red Lake hawking a sketch at the Snake Pit
                                        Lounge
                                for a quart of beer

Or bent over a table
in the basement   of Okanski's What-Not-Shop
unrolling a sheet of kraft paper

Or upstairs in his room above the Sears store

surrounded by the smile of a hundred paintings

Maybe he sees himself waking up with his wife on Mackenzie Island
the walls of their house   painted   like a canvas
and thinking LIFE IS GOOD
little Victoria and her baby brother in the next room Or

Maybe

he's back in Toronto at Pollock Gallery
at his first show   YELLING   about greed and deceit
startling onlookers
in a white-tabled restaurant
   Maybe he's drugged and naked
with a beautiful Italian boyfriend   Maybe   he's drunk in Vancouver
in a smoke-filled room
                    the skin melting off his back

But he's had his share of pain
      and he tries to avoid such scenes
before setting down on solid ground

This time he's painting in Tom Thomson's shack
at the McMichael Gallery,

and it reminds him of his CHILDHOOD
at Sand Point

He can already hear his grandparents speaking
                    in their ANISHINABEMOWIN
the kerosene lamp and woodstove throwing a soft glow
across the log cabin   GOODNESS DISTILLED

He is safe and warm listening to the rhythm of their

F e a t h e r – F a n   V o i c e s

                    Outside, first snow glistens
                        as his little finger traces
                    shadows on the wall beside him
                He pulls a piece of charcoal out of the fire
                    uses it to make a few tentative drawings
                        on a piece of cardboard
                    Watches curiously as the image
        begins to snake in the flickering light   and take on the weight
                        of his grandfather's stories
                            and become full

PAINTINGS large and luminous as Lake Nipigon
unfathomable PAINTINGS
in homes and galleries
around the country
and the world

Morrisseau is

everywhere

AND nowhere

Norval Morrisseau is among the first artists in Canada to take on the subject of
sexuality in his work, and the Toronto Star *was quick to note it in their headline:*
"Fiery Mother Earth reclining wantonly, gritty evidence of the artist's sexuality."

⊕

Artist in Union with Mother Earth, 1972

Sometimes when he wakes, his cock
so hard and so big
    an enormous red pine
    the kind every animal in the world
    floated on
    during the Great Flood,
he has no choice but to paint his wet dreams.

The artist laid over his subject
reclined and entwined. Becoming her.
Arms. Legs. Breasts. Thighs.
    His eyes the look of raw.
    Her eyes the look of ready.
The instant of entering stopped
(a hummingbird at a feeder)
and held in a touch
of pigment: earth and flesh and semen,
          blood and grass and water.

Union of Norval as Artist,
and Harriet as Mother Earth.
Cracked open like an egg
hitting a sizzling
skillet.

There are several versions of this painting, which shows green serpents writhing out of the orifices of a male figure. Christianity is one of Norval Morrisseau's major influences, and the references to it and his struggles with his on-going addictions and excessive lifestyle are apparent.

⊕

Self-Portrait. Devoured by His Own Passion, 1974

His snake passion eats him alive.
Rubbing alcohol.
Wine & whisky. Gallons of it.
A goddamn boatload.
Guzzling sloppy. Fat tongue
bloated like a bloodsucker.
Marihuana. Cocaine. Tranquillizers.
Mind dulled like a black eye.
Teeth sharpened like a blade
at the neck
of another lover:
female, male, between. It makes
no difference.

Morrisseau does his damnedest to turn off guilt
and become the consummate trickster,
Nanaboozho wrestling the world of the senses,
but his penis grows like a vine
writhing into a bouquet
of serpents
threatening
to strangle him.
And he is left with a Christian confession,
a portrait of his own
eternal
struggle.

Norval Morrisseau's grandmother Veronique was a devout Catholic and the artist himself attended a Catholic Residential School. He spoke of brainwashing and confusion when asked about Christianity. Critics have pointed to the influence of stained glass and religious imagery on his painting.

⊕

Indian Jesus Christ, 1974

Once again he is the blessed child
in the midst of adoration, exaltation:
Our Father Who Art in Heaven.
As his knees grind into the wood floor
and a throbbing ache moves up his legs
and drips off his upper lip,
into his cupped hands.

Staring up to the stained-glass Christ
above the priest and altar
he tries to focus on the one ray of light
filtering through halo and flame
like the divine spirit Himself
so that he might rise up to the rafters
and beyond into cool heaven.

The prayer for salvation never comes to pass.
Christ and his legion of angels
never once lift the roof off the chapel,
carry him up in a chorus of halleluiahs.
Morrisseau is left to find his own wings
and he does, painting his own remembering,
his hands bursting into holy acrylic pain.

The concept of power is central to the Ojibway belief system. When the artist underwent his vision quest and the spirit of a powerful Mukwa or Bear came to him, it became his doodem, *or totemic spirit guide. Morrisseau never stopped painting images of the Bear spirit throughout his career.*

⊕

Sacred Medicine Bear, 1974

When he prays he prays to Mukwa.
Not to a bear
but BEAR.
Life Spirit.
One & more
than one.
The eye of perception
pried open in youth
he is always the boy
who lay before *him*
all those years ago
supplicant
& fearful.

Mukwa, roused on hind legs
nose up sniffing
the arrogant nature
of human stink.
He recognizes the boy
& laughs
a hearty laugh
at the pitiful thing
who doesn't realize
his greatest fear
is his own
making.

Until much later
when
the boy-man

grows out of his short sight
& paints
himself
with a Bear head
and a sacred medicine bag
around his neck, inside
cobalt, azure, magenta
rose red, lemon yellow,
all the beauty of creation.
Until he finally sees
Who he is.
Where
he is going.

*A major subject of Norval Morrisseau's work, the thunderbird held great
significance for him. In his book* Legends of My People, The Great Ojibway
*(1965), in a chapter called "Thunderbird Beliefs," he writes, "The Ojibways of
the Lake Nipigon area believed in two kinds of thunderbird, one had an ordinary
bill, or beak, the other had a long, crooked beak. The latter had a very bad temper,
made the loudest noise and destroyed Indians by lightning...."*

⊕

Angry Thunderbird, 1975

Of the old stories. The belief in wings of thunder
and eyes of lightning.

You wrapped comfortably in the style of the moment.
Secure in the civilization of your apartment.

This flat image of what seems a bird with a small sack
of something. Electric eyes. Divided circles.

This is your mind on the mid-day road when the sky turns
black and you are suddenly no longer secure or certain.

Because for all your education you still tuck fear
under your pillow and rest your head on it every night.

And for a moment its scream lifts you high above your knowing
into the claws of something huge, immense.

Although Norval Morrisseau's work appears immune to political influences, this rare painting is explicitly political. It is also a painting that he never completes; in the upper corner is a faint circle penciled-in but never coloured.

⊕

The Gift, 1975

This one he never completes.

Maybe his hand goes numb.
Maybe it cramps each time he tries.
Maybe it turns into a fist.
Maybe it grabs a bottle.

The hopelessness is just too much.

He closes his eyes and wakes up.
All around the dead and dying.
Faces consumed by scab and pus.
Fire turned to smoke and ash.

He tries to translate his vision to canvas.

Manages a pockmarked priest,
and a pockmarked father embraced
by a benevolent handshake.
The exchange red as Christ-mass,
red as plague.
A pockmarked boy stares at a crucifix.
Even the next generation is not spared.
They are all infected by religion.

Little wonder why.

This is one of the first paintings Norval Morrisseau did of significant scale. It was done at a time when he and his wife, Harriet Kakegamic, were breaking up. Morrisseau spoke of finding refuge in the dream world, which resulted in this painting where the four figures surround the artist like female apostles.

⊕

The Artist and His Four Wives, 1975

After turning into a wounded bear – his madness a knot
to hang myself – he finds himself sprawled on a couch
holding up his hands to examine them. How can something
that does so much good do so much harm? He'd cut them off
but he needs them to paint.

He would weep but he knows it would do no good.

She has left him for another man who doesn't drink like him.
So he goes for a walk in the bush, and the pace turns into meditation.
Hours later he's still walking, begging the Creator for mercy.
Exhausted
he can sense a vision coming on like a shot of whisky.

It comes on so strong it makes him stagger.

He lies down on a bed of leaves and dreams
of an open prairie, a flat grassland. The year is 1600.
Four Assiniboine women come to him bright as TV.
They are delicately dressed in fringed deer hide. The vision
is so vivid he can see the white stitching, the blue porcupine quills.
Our husband, they tell him,

> we have come to make you happy
> we have come to give you comfort
> we have come to uplift your spirit
> we have come to sing you medicine.

It takes him 30 minutes to paint *The Artist and His Four Wives.*

It features a young wife in tears beside him as his other wives look on
pleading for him to stay. Thunderbird and Bear sentinels support the panel
as they support him. Everyone calls it spectacular at 43 × 131 inches.

When asked about it, he says he painted exactly what he saw:
love and healing. A vision that comforted him and made him so happy
all his bitterness and resentment, hurt and disappointment, vanished
like smoke curling from a stone bowl. How is it possible, you ask?

In one of Norval Morrisseau's few direct statements about "Mother Earth," he concludes that because we are all children of the earth, we are all one in spirit. Morrisseau saw his paintings as a unifying force regardless of culture or race. This painting is also another example of the artist foregrounding sexuality.

⊕

Mother Earth, 1975

As the earth
is in constant
motion
so woman is
in constant
creation
procreation
making all life
possible

This mother
an embodiment
of warm sensual touch
black tendril hair
crowned in colour,
as she sits cross-legged
red vagina
exposed
divided
a molten-bright
vulva

Golden breasts
full and ready
to be suckled
by all the children
of the world
gathered around her
like the other-than-humans
her own arm

turning into
a bird
because she is
who they are

Above her
brilliant
father sun
life heat
cobalt yellow
life seed
in the eyes of the beholder
reflecting
a unifying gesture
captured
in the throes
of catching
balance.

In this painting, bear, bird, fish and snake represent the sky, land—above and below — and water; they are entwined so that the composition is almost abstract. The artist connects these four creatures with black lines of communication that suggest the inherent interdependence of all living things.

⊕

Nature's Balance, 1975

Bear Bird Fish Snake
Worlds woven together,
teeth and eyes,
paws and claws,
fangs and scales
intricate as a sweetgrass basket.
Not a thing to be expelled.
Feared. Destroyed.
Life is the thing. How
the body knows.

In one of Morrisseau's few political paintings, he emphasizes that the treaties between the First Nations and the Euro-Canadians have not been honoured. He connects this disregard by the dominant culture to the treatment of the land.

⊕

The Land (Land Rights), 1976

This painting he doesn't whip up for money.
It's the furthest thing from his mind.
Something else
is going on here.

He begins by separating the canvas
into two spaces. Two paths
much like a wampum belt.

> One side blue for ocean.
> One side red for sunset.
> One side for Indian.
> One side for Whiteman.

On the Indian side, a man, the older generation,
sits with a howling baby on his lap.
A talking beaver balanced on his head like a totem.
Below his feet birds and fish support him.
The whole natural world inside him.
Behind him, the faces of the ancestors
facing backwards to the treaties.

> Look at them, the man is saying, Look at this,
> but his words do not cross the divide
> and go unheard.

The child strikes out toward two white-faced Canadians
startled by the cries curling from his mouth,
by his fist nearly the size of his head
punching through to their side.

The animals too protest the destruction
the settlers have brought with them.
Together they are saying when the earth dies
we all die. It is something
the artist wants you to see. Clearly,
like a glass of drinking water.

In an attempt to quit drinking, Morrisseau immersed himself in the teachings of Eckankar. His journey into the psychic world of soul travel resulted in paintings that introduced rebirth, hopefulness and spiritual potential to his work.

⊕

Spiritual Self Emerges, 1976

It's the threshold, the moment of purge.
The world of putrid gray impotence. Flushed.

What he aims for is the ability to say No
more, the power to pull his parched tongue back
into his mouth, peace at long last.

And he looks for it in Eckankar. The ancient science
of soul travel. In a new way of looking back.

    Astral planes. Inner master. Inner dimensions.
    Deep dreaming. Past lives. Higher worlds.

And for the first time a pale psychic blue appears
in his paintings much like snow's shadow at dawn.

A figure bejeweled, crowned,
his human potential coming to light
as his spiritual self emerges
signaling optimism for a wondrous future
in Ochre Gold, Titanium White, Scarlet Red.

Glossed over scars that slide under his skin
like worms.

*Norval Morrisseau said that he longed to do something great. By 1976 he is in a
state of self-imposed exile from his family and living in Winnipeg. As he prepares
for the show at Pollock Gallery in Toronto, he plunges into* Man Changing Into
Thunderbird (Transmigration) *with complete confidence. Many critics claim this
to be his greatest work, and proof of his genius.*

⊕

Man Changing Into Thunderbird (Transmigration), 1977

From the very first time he heard the story about the man who changed
into a thunderbird, Morrisseau has wanted to paint it. But as yet he has
had no idea how to squeeze the essence of it onto canvas. How does one
go about doing something so daunting? As early as 1964 he pondered this
question, noting that such large works would require much thought to
concentrate the story pictorially. It is something that haunts him, dangles
in front of him, gets caught in the dream catcher web of a spider, escapes
through a hole in the night sky and slides down a path of owl feathers
into the world of myth and creation.

> *The story says there were seven brothers. One day*
> *the youngest Wahbi Ahmik*
> *went hunting and met a beautiful woman*
> *named Nimkey Banasik.*
> *They fell in love at first sight*
> *and the young warrior took her home to his wigwam*
> *where they lived as man and wife*
> *and were happy.*
> *All the brothers cherished her except one*
> *Ahsin, the oldest,*
> *who felt only hatred for her.*

The idea grows inside Morrisseau the way a butterfly grows inside a
chrysalis. Except it is not about a butterfly, it is about a thunderbird, and
more about a whole way of seeing, about perception and belief. When it
finally cracks open, or rather when he cracks it open, the idea is so large
he knows instinctively it will be one of his most important pieces. Not
junk commercialism done for a quick buck. Not twenty paintings on a

clothesline, him jumping between them like a jackrabbit. Not another set of nesting loons or another multicoloured trout. Not something he can paint with his eyes half closed. Half in stupor. Once in the moment his eyes are wide open and burning with possibility, as though giant talons are digging into his memory and stirring his imagination. As though clamped onto his shoulder muscles, with the steady beat of locomotive wings, they are lifting him high above the ground.

> *One day Wahbi Ahmik returned from hunting*
> *and discovered the campfire near his wigwam*
> *stained in blood.*
> *Panic-stricken, he rushed to his wife*
> *but discovered her gone.*
> *Knowing what his brother Ahsin felt for her*
> *he stormed into his tent*
> *and demanded to know what had happened.*
> *I see a trail of blood leading into the forest.*
> *What have you done?*

By this time Morrisseau is again showing with the Pollock Gallery in Toronto, but he is hardly under Jack Pollock's tutelage, their artist – agent relationship strained by their giant personalities. With his home in Red Lake far behind him, Morrisseau is lapping up the good life like a saucer of sweet milk. And his art has become little more than a means to an end, more commerce than calling. He sells it to buy the basics like cigarettes, groceries (though he eats little for a man his size), shoes or a shirt when he needs it. More often than not he simply trades paintings for whatever he needs or wants, a week's rent in a flop house, a bottle, a meal, an English Derby plate, a Spode teapot, a blowjob, a fuck, everything and anything. The moment the only thing that matters.

> *Ahsin was not afraid of his younger brother's anger.*
> *You brought this woman Nimkey Banasik to our village.*
> *We were all happy together before she came.*
> *Now she is gone for good.*
> *When you left this morning I sent our other brothers away*
> *to be alone with her.*
> *Then I saw her cooking for you*
> *and I got out my sharpest arrow*

which found its mark in her hip.
I would have chased her down and killed her
if not for the roar of thunder
that filled the sky
and frightened me.

As for Pollock, he is still smarting from the Kenora court case a few years earlier—though he knows Morrisseau didn't instigate it. By this time Pollock's gallery and personal life are in shambles, his brazen honesty and vanity making him *persona non grata* in what he calls Toronto's bitchy art scene. His life of flirting with excess has scarred both his body and mind, inside and outside. So honest and vain he later admits in his own book, printed in England where nobody knows him personally, that if he were to drop dead tomorrow the single most important thing he would be remembered for is the art of Norval Morrisseau.

Oh Ahsin! My foolish brother, cried Wahbi Ahmik.
Even though I am mad enough to kill you
I pity you.
Did it not ever cross your mind who Nimkey Banasik was?
You must know her name means Thunderbird Woman.
I would have told you
if not for your blind hatred.
I would have also told you
she had six sisters.
Can you not imagine the power our children would have had?
What it would have meant for all of us.
For this woman was a thunderbird
in human form.
And now it is too late.

To say that Morrisseau is Pollock's cash cow and he is only in it for the money would be unfair, unless you put it in perspective and add that Morrisseau is everyone's cash cow. No, safe to say there is something more between them. For Morrisseau, their initial meeting was no accident. There is no room for accidents, or luck for that matter, in his belief system.

I am leaving to never return until I find this woman
Wahbi Ahmik said, as he turned his back on his brother

and followed the blood trail
that led far into the great forest.
For many moons he travelled until he came to a huge mountain
that reached over the clouds and beyond.
And he began to climb higher and higher
Until the earth disappeared and he reached the summit.
And there before him on a blanket of cloud
stood a towering teepee
shooting forth
lightning
and thunder
across the sky.

To be sure, whatever Morrisseau and Pollock's frailties, together they are magnificent. As if they walk on clouds. Pollock routinely reads Morrisseau's mind like a cup of tea leaves and reminds him of his purpose and stature, prodding and coaxing to get the best out of him.

From the majestic edifice came the laugher of women
which suddenly stopped.
For they felt his presence.
Then the teepee flap opened and there stood Nimkey Banasik
looking more beautiful than ever.
With concern she asked why he had followed her.
Because you are my life, he answered.
She smiled upon hearing his words
and beckoned him forward.
Come inside, she said,
and we will give you the power
to walk on clouds.

Pollock knows Morrisseau can handle scale, which he has proven in *The Artist and His Four Wives* and *Some of My Friends*, each of them marvelous at 43 by 131 inches. What he doesn't know is that Morrisseau has also done sets of paintings, diptychs, like *Merman and Merwoman*, and has played with perspective in *The Land (Land Rights),* where he divided the canvas into two panes. The problem is, Morrisseau is back living in Winnipeg, which makes it impossible for Pollock to keep track of him. Pollock knows the challenge is not to keep him painting, which he does constantly, but to make sure that Morrisseau sends the gallery what he does, as he would just as likely sell to anyone who comes knocking on his door.

> *Inside the wigwam were seated two old thunderbirds*
> *in human form.*
> *Light radiated from their eyes*
> *suggesting a presence full of power and wisdom.*
> *Immediately they saw Wahbi Ahmik's hunger*
> *and offered him food.*
> *In an instant a roar of deafening thunder erupted*
> *as they stretched out their arms and changed into thunderbirds*
> *and flew away*
> *to return with a big horned snake with two heads and three tails.*
> *They offered it to Wahbi Ahmik to eat*
> *but he quickly turned away from the writhing mass of flesh.*
> *The next morning they again asked him if he needed food*
> *and the thunderbirds returned with a black snake sturgeon*
> *and later with a cat-like demigod.*
> *And Wahbi Ahmik grew weaker*
> *and weaker.*

Pollock flies back and forth between Toronto and Winnipeg, making sure that Morrisseau is not going astray and taking whatever paintings the artist has finished. Bob Checkwitch of Great Grasslands Graphics is also working with Morrisseau during this time doing a series of prints, and helps to keep him in check. Through meetings, telephone calls and letters, Morrisseau and Pollock talk over the concept for *Man Changing into Thunderbird (Transmigration)*, and after much discussion Morrisseau decides to translate the story into panels. He knows this will be his greatest work to date.

> *Finally the old woman who feared that Wahbi Ahmik was starving*
> *told her daughter to take him*
> *to her great medicine uncle*
> *Southern Thunderbird*
> *whom she knew would have strong medicine for the human.*
> *They laid Wahbi Ahmik on a blanket of cloud*
> *softer than rabbit fur and wrapped him gently*
> *so that he would not see.*

And with the thunder suddenly erupting
Wahbi Ahmik felt his nest of cloud move.
After what seemed like a mere moment
they stopped
and his wife Nimkey Banasik
removed the cloud from around him.
And there in front of Wahbi Ahmik
perched on a cloud
stood a great medicine lodge.

Three weeks before the opening of the exhibition, which is scheduled for August 10 at two o'clock, Morrisseau sends four panels to Toronto. Pollock's constant nudging has been well worth it: the complex multicoloured thunderbird-man against the brilliant orange background in a shrine of the natural world almost vibrates off the canvas. It is a feast for the eyes. But after staring at the images Pollock realizes that Morrisseau has yet to complete the story. Morrisseau tells him not to worry, the man will be transformed into thunderbird. Another two weeks pass and Pollock starts to become anxious. He telephones Winnipeg and Morrisseau assures him that he will bring the last two panels to Toronto with him. Pollock warns him that he needs time to prepare the paintings—they have to be stretched and framed. Again Morrisseau tells him not to worry.

Wahbi Ahmik looked around him and saw many lodges
the homes of many different kinds of thunderbirds
all in human form.
Entering the great medicine lodge
Nimkey Banasik brought her uncle greetings from her mother
and beseeched him for help.
My mother said that you would have medicine for my husband
so that he may eat as we do
and perhaps even become one of us.
The old thunderbird stood in silence, pondering the love between them
and the consequences
of such an action.
Let it be known that if this human takes my medicine
he will never return to earth
but will become a thunderbird forever.

Then the medicine thunderbird took two small blue medicine eggs
mixed them together
and advised Wahbi Ahmik to drink the liquid.

On Friday, August 9, Morrisseau saunters into the gallery about lunchtime. Under his arm is the roll that Pollock is expecting. Everyone takes a break from installing the show and gathers around to see that last two panels. Morrisseau grins as he unrolls two blank canvases. Pollock is stunned. It's the last straw. He barks and growls at Morrisseau, who calmly tells him that the pictures will be finished in time for the show. Pollock exclaims that the other panels are still at the framer's and he won't be able to use them for reference. No problem, Morrisseau says, unmoved by the calamity that Pollock foresees.

The moment the potion entered Wahbi Ahmik
he felt a strange power surge throughout his body.
Looking at his hands and feet he saw
they were no longer human
but the claws and wings of a thunderbird.
With the next drink the change was complete.
He was now a thunderbird.
His human form, the wigwams, the great medicine lodge
all disappeared.
Everyone was now a thunderbird
inhabiting the realm of thunderbirds.
And so Wahbi Ahmik and Nimkey Banasik
thanked Southern Thunderbird
and flew home together
where Wahbi Ahmik feasted
on thunderbird food
and lived out his life with this beloved wife Nimkey Banasik.

Morrisseau purchases three brushes and about twenty tubes of paint from Daniel's Art Supplies up the street from his hotel. For the life of him Pollock cannot fathom how Morrisseau is going to execute the paintings, and asks himself how the artist can possibly carry in his head the complete chromatic palette of the first four panels. As Pollock is leaving the hotel room, Morrisseau tells him to come back at one o'clock in the morning and he'll have the paintings ready for him. Not knowing what to expect, Pollock returns at the exact hour. Morrisseau swings open the door to his room and there they are, spread out on the floor. He has finished the series with two more panels. The moment Pollock sees them it becomes clear to him that Morrisseau has not only successfully recreated the colours of the first four panels, but he has somehow managed to match their composition and scale. They are exactly like the others.

And the people who remained below
in the world of humans
generation upon generation
remember Wahbi Ahmik
as the Man Who Changed
into
a Thunderbird.

With the canvases still wet, Pollock carries them back to the gallery in his outstretched arms and brings them to the framer's the moment they are dry. The show opens on time, with Morrisseau touching up the new panels with dabs of paint on the tip of his right index finger. Within one hour the complete set of six panels is sold. And as Pollock predicted, everyone who is witness to *Man Changing into Thunderbird (Transmigration)* cannot look away. As one reviewer describes it, the brilliant stained-glass colours and the visionary fluidity of its tangled shapes give the work a joyous force that overwhelms. Only later will Morrisseau confess to the press, saying I didn't think I'd finish it, and then add, displaying his customary confidence, I had a right to see all those visions. I am a shaman. I am part thunderbird. It is me.

After Norval Morrisseau's death in 2007, controversy erupted over the authenticity of his paintings. Did he really do thousands? Morrisseau's own erratic lifestyle and laissez-faire attitude about the "business of art" set the stage for the origin of this controversy.

⊕

Untitled (Abomination), 1977

As though he were slipping into an underworld.
Before him a canvas of hospital green,
a glass slide under a microscope,
a petri dish of amoeba
fish-tail figures, jagged teeth
prehistoric saucer eyes.

       An abomination, he is quoted saying.
       Fakes. Forgeries. Awful things.
       The greatest fraud in Canadian art history.
       Completely lacking in provenance.

By now he is frail and sick,
his hands shake uncontrollably,
a huge bear-of-a-man
shrunken in a wheelchair
like a wrinkled scrotum,
the stink of death and legacy on his mind.

       And what of Morrisseau's signature
       scrawled in black paint and authenticated
       by a top forensic document examiner
       and handwriting analysis expert?
       What of the DNA certainty?

There was a time Morrisseau didn't give a good goddamn
about such inconsequential human matters.
Up on his hind legs. Snorting and drinking
and fucking the night away.

Nights so dark he couldn't see
or feel what he was signing
if it smacked him in the face.

Norval Morrisseau did this painting in honour of his grandfather Potan. By the mid-1970s, Morrisseau was desperate to stop drinking and used the new-age movement Eckankar, with its emphasis on past lives, dreams and soul travel, to help him recover. From this point on, he began to include both Anishinaabe and Eckankar influences in the painting.

⊕

The Storyteller: The Artist and His Grandfather, 1978

I

Knowledge passed on.
Daebaudjimod
Grandfather Wise man Story teller
Debon
Spirit of Winter
A time for the telling
Manitous. Demi-gods
Gathering. Listening
In the arms of Grandfather Thunder
Epingishmook Winohah
Mudjeekawis Papeekawis Chibiabos Nanaboozho
Listen!
The rattle of bones in the trees
The flying skeleton man
Paugauk
Listen!
The scrape of claws on the rock
The flesh-eating cannibals
Windigo
Listen!
The imprint of scales in the sand
Mishipesheu.
Listen, my grandson!
All around you
Inside you.

II

A baby's conscious
Connection
Original thought
Ancient belief
Medicine Dream
Six layers of Creation
Four for the Indians
One for the Whiteman
One for the Creator – Legions of Spirits
Grandfather Thunder spirit guide
Transformation
ECK
New Language for a New Age
Six Worlds
Becoming
Seven Planes
The mind's eye
Energy at the subatomic level.
Karma
Psychic state.
HU.
Love Song.
Breath
Soul Travel
Child becomes Shaman.
Child becomes WoMan
The colours of healing
Red Breath. Pink Breath. Orange Breath
Yellow Breath. Green Breath. Baby Blue Breath
Midnight Blue Breath. Turquoise Breath. Violet Breath. Purple Breath
Arrival: the House of Invention.

Of his seven children, Victoria is the one child whom the artist really helped raise and got to know. He spoke of her often and did a number of paintings of her. When she was in her early teens, she and her father travelled to Curve Lake Reserve near Peterborough to visit a friend, who recalled, "You could tell that Norval really loved his daughter."

⊕

Victoria and Family, 1978

I

His oldest daughter Victoria has just had a baby
And he can react in only one way.
He pictures everything he wishes for her.
A suckling child in the embrace
Of a loving mother, a protective robe,
A proud father, birds connecting
To the sky world, a radiant halo,
The divine love of parenthood.

He keeps his mind focused
On this sacred birthing moment.
We can learn how to heal with colour,
He thinks, laying Naphthol Red over
Cadmium Yellow as he dresses the figures
With the power of the spectrum.
Cobalt Blue streams from the woman's hair
Into a circle of life-giving connection.

He dips his brush into a jar of pigment
And begins again, embroidering the figures
In the leaves of a Learning Tree,
Berries of knowledge,
Butterflies of happiness,
His ever-vigilant spirit birds
Watching with their bright eyes.
Together all the humble creatures of the earth,
Insect, bird, human, joined in kinship
To a simple happy family.

II

You never forget the first one. You hold her tiny
in your cupped hands. Look down at her
and she is gone. Just like that. For the rest of your life.

Her first pair of shoes. Her doll with one button eye.
All she brought with her. Gone. In her absence you say a prayer.
You pray she is safe. You pray she makes the right choices.

When you do see her on the occasional visit you feel her breath
On your cheek as though you were swaddling her for the first time
but by now she is an adult with her own first-born.

The people you introduce her to see your love glowing
like a Byzantine halo, and they say it is as real as the paintings
you do of her. It is beyond doubt.

They are also surprised when you pause to speak softly
of tone, composition, colour. To see it coming from you
who long ago perfected the art of leaving.

The artist synthesizes traditional Ojibway beliefs with the "religion" of Eckankar
to create a unique visual language. The image of a multicoloured thunderbird
appears as though inlaid with pieces of tile or glass on a background of vibrant
blue, symbolizing spiritual rebirth.

⊕

Astral Thunderbird, 1978

His Inner Master guides him
to higher consciousness.
A spiritual helper,
a dreamtime
he learns to call upon
as a loon calls in evening.

Beyond the physical universe of objects
weighted and measured.
Outside the realm of electrons
and neurons,
chemically charged synapses.

Like a Buddha he sits at the genesis of consciousness
Embodied as a brilliant thunderbird

He is quick to speak
with his new vocabulary
pressed into him like a leaf.
Of Astral Visions, House of Invention,
Seventh Plane, Deep Dreaming.

And the unbelievable becomes believable.
Faith is everything.
Proof in a brush of colour
that can heal anyone
but himself.

In his books Legends of My People *(1965) and* Windigo and Other Tales
of the Ojibway *(1969) Norval Morrisseau speaks about the dreaded Windigo
with its insatiable greed and appetite for human flesh. Illustrating one of the
foundational stories of the Anishinaabe oral tradition, he paints a huge ghastly
figure with a shock of white hair, razor-sharp teeth and claws.*

⊕

Windigo, 1979

White-haired giant stuffing his sharp mouth, his greedy guts
an oily ocean.

Sometimes a hard night cracks the shore in the high sun, a fissure
erupts, and the artist finds himself plastered to sand.

Greed. Gluttony. The vices of our age turned into virtues.
Read all about it: white-collar thieves turned into porn stars.

Sometimes he sits on a bench with an empty bottle of fuel
and weeps into his hands.

The faint crunch of bone. Always there gnawing at something
or someone just behind the scene.

Sometimes he hears it. Inside himself. Growling
for more gut rot. For forgetting.

500 years of blood and booze, politicians and police, and a stinking pit
of bodies the size of the world.

Sometimes his face is false. A false face carved from a living tree trunk.
Its crazy grin warning him to beware.

The salivating tongue of human-kind. A red flag stuffed into his mouth,
your mouth, and pulled out and out and out.

*"As far as sex was concerned, I did everything under the sun." Norval
Morrisseau's exploits, like many stories of Nanabush/Nanaboozho, the Ojibway
trickster figure, are explicitly sexual and ribald. In these stories Nanabush is taught
a lesson, or teaches a lesson, while learning something about himself, as we learn
something about human nature.*

$$\oplus$$

The Other Side of the Shaman, 1979

One day Nanabush's pecker grows red-pine high,
So he decides to relieve himself with a little white lie.

With such a huge burden he has nothing to lose,
And comes up with what he thinks is a pretty good ruse.

And so he drags that big uncomfortable thing around
Until he finally reaches the nearest town.

> The evil Windigos are coming, he begins to shout,
> As the people panic, not knowing what it's about.
> Quick, bend over, and we'll give them a scare.
> It's my shaman's secret that I'm willing to share.
> Up go the skirts and down come the pants
> While Nanabush aims his mammoth lance.
> Of course they are all eager to agree
> When they see his package is as big as a tree.
> Every young woman and man in this way he deflowers.
> Skipping along, he laughs and sings, I've got the power!

Today we hear such a story and we are aghast
And we ask ourselves, was that really the past?

Some will say he deserves to be hung up by a testicle.
While others say it's all in the name of fun and spectacle.

After prohibition comes a forest of sex.
After excess what comes next?

Norval Morrisseau moved from condemning homosexuality to embracing it. This reflects not so much his own sexual awakening but rather his break from Catholic indoctrination and his disregard for societal attitudes. This painting shows two male lovers with entwined penises that look like caterpillars, while another caterpillar frames the image, symbolizing that all life is in the midst of transformation.

⊕

Indian Erotic Fantasy, n.d.

The first thing that comes to mind is not the painting.
Instead, it makes you see the other world.
Where people like them are not worthy of God.
Where they are dragged away and stoned, or chained in a cellar
to become play for the torturer's tools. Where death is too good
for creatures holding to unnatural acts.

Only then do you see
the painting: two men holding hands
holding a valentine heart
Penises engorged
entwined
and staring
at each other
eyes like the caterpillar
that encircles them
Symbol of
transformation
that everything
in the world
is in the midst
of change
everything connected
to the circle of life
that floats like purple clouds
around the two love-locked figures.

These men, not heterosexual, homosexual, bisexual,
but rather Agokwa, between male and female.

Known since the beginning of time
and whom the artist celebrates in his erotic fantasy
where men wear necklaces bright as the sun
and red and pink power erupts in a geyser
of pure pleasure.

MOTHER OF ALL THINGS

Despite the hardships in his life, Norval Morrisseau's paintings exhibit a tone of optimism expressed through theme, colour and composition. Black lines of communication connect the figures in this painting, and we see a baby suckling the breast of Mother Earth while a panoply of creatures gather around wide-eyed.

⊕

Mother of All Things, 1980

bear bird child
suckles earth mother
all is well

After Norval Morrisseau left his wife Harriet in Red Lake, he rarely saw his seven children, and his family was left to fend for themselves. Morrisseau's behaviour and inaction is characterized as irresponsible and callus, but the artist never forgot his children, constantly painting them in an environment of love and happiness.

⊕

Child with Flowers, 1980

When he thinks of his seven children
he thinks of flowers, a whole field of them,
sunrise red and sunset pink and sky blue
petals shimmering in the painterly light.

And so he paints them as the babies
they once were: Victoria, David, Pierre,
Eugene, Christian, Michael, Lisa
over and over again.

Each child happy as a butterfly. Each one
held forever in his arms. Life as fragrant
and sweet as a flower just beyond
their reach.

Since his first solo show at Pollock Gallery on September 12, 1962, Norval
Morrisseau's work has never stopped selling. He is one of the most popular painters
in the history of Canadian art. Although Morrisseau paints out of his own
Ojibway culture, his work clearly holds universal appeal.

⊕

We Are All One, 1981

This one he does with you
in mind. We can all be Indian
but soon forget,
he says. Which makes
you wonder, What can
he possibly mean?

Bird, bear, fish,
fashioned like a halo
to a child's head,
all growing together
in a garden
where nobody
or anything
is ever expelled.

When Norval Morrisseau left his wife Harriet in Red Lake, she moved up with the children to Sandy Lake where she could find help from her family. Eventually she charged the artist with abandonment.

⊕

The Children, 1982

The last stroke of the brush makes him weep.
He's feeling sorry for himself again, and
there's not a damn thing you can do about it.
You don't even want to try. Frankly, when
he gets like this you don't even want to be
near him.

•

Your son wraps his velvet arms around your neck
and whispers in his small damp breath
that he loves you, and at that instant his words
are a healing balm with the power to mend
the rent in the world.

•

He pins the painting to a kitchen clothesline
to let it dry. A little boy and a little girl
in a landscape of pink birds and red blossoms.
Father sun, constant and giving, lights the cadmium sky
like grace, a dream of pure undiluted goodness.

•

Sometimes when your son falls or simply
cries because he cannot have what he wants
it is your turn to put your arms around him and
carry him to a den of soft grass. Where together
you become bear, deer, wolf, fox.

•

He will make an effort to see his children
but not often. And yet he will spend his life
painting them. The purity of his effort
will ball into rage, leaving behind
broken glass, broken walls, broken people.

One of Norval Morrisseau's masterpieces, Androgyny *was donated by the artist to the Canadian people on April 15, 1983. Twenty-five years later, it was moved from the lobby of the Department of Indian and Northern Affairs to the Governor General's Rideau Hall Ballroom. While honouring the artwork and the artist, this gesture has been nevertheless controversial in light of Canada's disregard for Indigenous rights.*

⊕

Androgyny, 1983

four panels assembled into one 366 x 610 cm canvas laid before him
ἀνδρόγυνος
a room dwarfed barely able to contain his vision the imagining
driving scale in waves unfolding a reverie painted on sky astral
horizon earth water under upper inner outer world sphere consciousness portal
androgynus
body mind spirit wisdom love bravery humility honesty respect truth
brother sister father mother grandfather grandmother friend lover family
anishininabek doodum nipigon sandpoint beardmore fish maang mukwa
berdache
animikibe bahnasik midewiwin grand medicine society goodhearted
mitigwakik jiissaskid shaking tent wabino serpent medicine
mikkinnuk pinasiwuk mishomis nokomis
two spirit
anishinaabemowin mishipeshu manidoo tobacco sage sweetgrass cedar
west death memory nagamon north south sunrise waaseyaaban birth
mitig flower butterfly joy east transformation grace ceremony power
niizh manidoowag
child shaman elder transcendence spring sun moon anang eternity
land history country rain language aadizookaan tradition prayer
eye wind beak claw sight message messenger cosmology vision
agokwe
body mind spirit symbol colour hue value intensity so vivid
the dreaming hurts
his eyes
wakes him
niibaadibik
in the middle of night

After a successful show in Santa Barbara, California, where he unwittingly took a drink of tequila, Norval Morrisseau lived on the streets of Vancouver for six months doing what the public came to call "boozy sketches" for a quick buck. Through it all—even when he looked as though on death's doorstep—he believed he would eventually sober up.

⊕

Ojibway Family Under the Tree of Life, 1987

These are the people
He wraps in healing flowers
And takes to bed
In his technicolour dreams.
Cuddles up to them
Every night
On the steel grates
Of Vancouver's streets.

Awakening,
He takes in the gray world
Before turning his back on it.
Rolling over to block it out
As long as humanly
Possible.
Before turning
Into something
Unimaginable.

Throughout his career, Norval Morrisseau was known to do up to thirty paintings
at a time. He would string them up on a clothesline or lay them out across a room
and bounce from painting to painting as he moved from colour to colour until they
were finished. This kind of painting angered Jack Pollock, who knew the artist
could do great things if he could manage his money, and hence his output.

$\oplus$

Spirit Helpers, 1988

Off the street.
Eating regularly.
Drinking irregularly.
Regaining his health.
The press announces "The Shaman's Return."
He agrees wholeheartedly
and attributes it to one thing:
his Spirit Helpers.

Over his career he paints a thousand
different versions of them:
bear & bird & fish.
To the point where he can do them
with his eyes closed.
And they become a quick fix
for ready cash.
To the point where they become a staple
like bread & pork & beans.

Norval Morrisseau never lost interest in sex and was often accompanied by either a young man or woman. He is known to have done stacks of erotic drawings and paintings. No other Canadian artist, Indigenous or Non-Indigenous, has a comparable body of work.

⊕

Untitled ("Norval's Dick Drawings"), 1990

That's what he calls them, tongue bright
as a prickly pear leaf dripping wet.
The moment stirring in his pants.
Crimson cock growing like a vine
or a striped serpent
slithering across the floor
poking into a juicy fat
bear's bum.

As for moose, his anus ain't what it used to be. Ha.

He's not shy to show them stacked inches thick.
Let alone draw them. Spontaneous drawings
quick as sex. Au contraire,
he's proud of everything he's done
and would do it over in a wink
of a mascara eye.
He mumbles, Ah the good old days.
As the young hooker
is escorted in.

Did Norval Morrisseau sexually abuse his oldest son when he was a boy? We
know the artist is alleged to have done bizarre things when he was drinking, such
as sitting a niece on a hot stove and painting with feces on the walls of a hotel
room. When asked about the time he spent at St. Joseph's Residential School in
Fort William (now Thunder Bay) he admitted that he was sexually abused there.

⊕

Untitled (Shaman Traveller to Other Worlds for Blessings), c. 1990s

More than anything he wants to purify himself.
Boil his flesh in a ceremony of water,

rock and steam.
Leave his body and fly away from the accusing
face of the world. Paint himself
into his beloved thunderbird perfect self
Sprout strong red wings, wise yellow eyes,
a pink mind, calm and sharp
as a beak. And fly with orange and purple birds
into a portal of brilliant space.
For good. For blessing.

No not me not me not me no not me not me not me

August 10, 1990. He picks up the newspaper like
any other day and there before his eyes
his oldest son in court for sexual abuse.
Saying he was abused
by his famous father for more than 11 years.
An emotional cripple, and the artist to blame,
says the judge. Another tragic chapter
in Norval Morrisseau's very tragic life,
he reads, and then turns back to his healing art,
in unwavering belief.

No to me to me to me to me to me to me to me to me

The origin stories of the Anishinaabek include the great migration, or
chibimoodaywin, which tells of seven prophets coming to the Ojibway people living
in the east and guiding them with the sacred megis shell to safety in the west.
Norval Morrisseau did numerous paintings based on this story. This version shows
four canoes, and in one of them is a family, and among the family is the artist
himself.

$\oplus$

The Great Migration, 1992

A story told and retold long before the tidal wave descended.
Of a time when the people stood in a storm of uncertainty
and prayed in uncertainty. Of a time when the spirits spoke
and warned of the coming invasion.

By now his health is gone.

What we see is canoe upon canoe heading west on a migration
of centuries. Families and clans s- t- r- e- t- c- h-e-d
by the thousands, searching for a new life,
birth, rebirth, transformation,
a community of human and other-than-human,
Anishinaabek, birds, bears, trees, all moving in unison, in beauty.

By now there is no room for darkness in his life.

In the gallery we speak so low the mice in the walls barely hear
us. We watch navigation and wish we understood the signs
that appear like rainbows before our eyes and open us to possibility.
The great sweet-water ocean where the pull of demi-gods is
unrelenting. We dip our heads into its blueness and stare for hours.
A yellow-eyed Medicine Snake swims alongside.

Happiness is a bouquet of butterflies, the ocean is emerald.

We know the people stop according to plan to paint
their journey on rock. We know four clans separate
to travel the four directions. We know they arrive

and survive to be born again. This we know
from the smiling children.

Guided by the shaman-artist, we witness a dream of faith.

One of Norval Morrisseau's most imaginative paintings, it signals a leap of creativity for the artist. He combines the tenets of Eckankar with his grandfather's tradition teachings. Circular motifs that have previously symbolized balance and were mostly restricted to the corners of a canvas now become central; here they are portals to another world or reality.

⊕

Observations of the Astral World, 1994

By the time he finally grinds to a halt
he is down on all fours swinging side to side.
He could wring out his body like an old rag
and have enough whiskey to fill a bottle.

A month of serpents licking his face,
sucking his brain, and his only hope
to summon his bear power
and paw his paintbrush back to life.

He closes his eyes and prays and in a burst
of everlasting light is in the midst of soul travel.
He sees a family, the same happy family
he always sees in this delicate dream.

They are entwined by the sacred tree of life
– in full bloom,
apples bright as red-lip kisses,
branches the shape of robins and bluebirds.

Grandparent, father, mother, child, observing
their spirit selves among the other-than-humans:
a bear, a bird, a fish, a man,
a bear-bird-fish-man.

The astral world projected like a map
of the mind, seven planes up
to a separate reality, where cement grey
does not exist and colour heals.

Where the moon is a portal
you can slip through. Watch!
As a school of fish appears and disappears
like children playing a game of hide and seek.

Eyes in the shape of an O. Mouths
saying Hello.
        Here I am.
Let me show you the way.

Norval Morrisseau connects the aesthetic of Anishinaabe floral patterns to storytelling. Emerging from the story tree's branches are his beloved birds, significant to the Ojibway within the doodum, or totemic clan system. It is a way of being and knowing in the world that is the antithesis of a system based on weight and measurement.

⊕

Ojibway Story Tree, 1996

His hand swims across the paper possessed
A divining rod detecting groundwater
A sacred cosmology

(Thunderbird Spirit. Astrophysics. Midewiwin Sacred Bear. Particle Physics. Astral Beings. Particle accelerator. Indian Jesus Christ. Molecular biology. The Virgin Mary. Quantum Chemistry. The Great Migration. Genetics.

Sacred Loons. Solar Neutrinos. Sunset Ceremony. Mathematical Logic. Ojibway Shaman Figure. Computational Complexity Theory.

Observations of the Astral World. Number Theory. Sacred Loons. Database. Shaman with Medicine Powers. Fractal Dimension. Keeper of Animals. Metric Expansion. The Grand Shaman. The Big Bang Theory.

Great Medicine Snake. The Observable Universe. Mishipisheu. The Hubble Space Telescope. Man Changing into Thunderbird)

His hand jumps to completion possessed
A geiger counter detecting ionizing radiation
A physical cosmology.

A few years after meeting Gabe Vadas on the streets of Vancouver in the late
1980s, Norval Morrisseau was introduced to Vadas' future wife, Michele Richard.
The couple eventually had two sons. Morrisseau lived with the family until he
required professional care due to Parkinson's disease.

⊕

A Tribute to My Beloved Daughter-in-law,
c.1995–96

Sometimes he feels the world
so intensely he finds himself
walking bare feet
on a path of razor quills,
and he has no choice but to paint
to steady himself.
More than once he has come close
to killing himself
gagged and retched up his rank guts
but it's not easy to die,
says the man with the stomach of iron.

Still he knows full well
the end of his earthly plane
is in sight – he has borne witness,
he has dreamed
an army of blank eyes
staring at him.
And he knows they will come in a swarm
and stake him
to the sweating ground,
eat his life
moment by moment
and there is nothing he can do about it.

By the time he paints his portrait
of Michele for looking after him –
for being what he is not –
he is staring straight

into the sun for inspiration.
And already he can see a scar
coming over the horizon
threatening
to blot him out.

What he paints is not out of the ordinary.
A simple canvas
of a young mother
and child
surrounded by faithful spirit birds
joyful butterflies.
a sacred story tree,
the same old images
transformed
and rebirthed
in brilliant yellow
red and magenta
as he tries to imagine
his arrival.

Drawn to Catholic imagery and faith, Norval Morrisseau reproduces a subject
he painted while in jail in Kenora in the 1970s. In his original painting Kateri
Tekakwitha, the Roman Catholic Saint, is clutching a crucifix. In this later version
the crucifix is absent. The saint is surrounded by the artist's signature floral pattern
and the presence of birds, indicating a higher spiritual plane.

⊕

Lily of the Mohawk, 1995–96

A chalice of wine, sacramental bread,
flesh and blood of Christ
that little puppies learn to lap up.
A seed planted
gripped succulently
around his sacred heart.
No matter how deep he digs,
cuts, hacks, burns.

The idea of forgiveness,
rebirth,
second chances,
so enticing he wants to bathe in
the white milk of it.
From pockmarked to radiant
unblemished like the face of God
Himself. An ending
he cannot live without.

By the end of the 1990s, Norval Morrisseau was fighting Parkinson's disease and confined to a wheelchair. Although he always said he was not restricted to the earthly realm, and constantly "soul travelled," toward the end of his life his hands shook uncontrollably and he struggled to paint.

⊕

Untitled (Thunderbird and Canoe in Flight, Norval on Scooter), c. 1990s

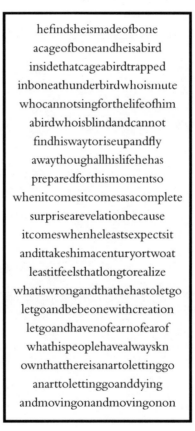

hefindsheismadeofbone
acageofboneandheisabird
insidethatcageabirdtrapped
inboneathunderbirdwhoismute
whocannotsingforthelifeofhim
abirdwhoisblindandcannot
findhiswaytoriseupandfly
awaythoughallhislifehehas
preparedforthismomentso
whenitcomesitcomesasacomplete
surprisearevelationbecause
itcomeswhenheleastsexpectsit
andittakeshimacenturyortwoat
leastitfeelsthatlongtorealize
whatiswrongandthathehastoletgo
letgoandbebeonewithcreation
letgoandhavenofearnofearof
whathispeoplehavealwayskn
ownthatthereisanartolettinggo
anarttolettinggoanddying
andmovingonandmovingonon

As Norval Morrisseau's Parkinson's disease progressed, his physical well-being deteriorated. In addition to seeking the help of Western doctors, he turned to alternative medicine and a myriad of herbal remedies and diets, but his health did not improve. He finally came to understand the nature of his illness through dream.

⊕

Medicine Man with Bear (The Poisoned Bear), 1996

In the old days when a shaman gave an Indian medicine, he often told a story – Morrisseau was given such a story he called The Poisoned Bear.

Morrisseau is living in the British Properties in West Vancouver when he gets sick – he goes to see a doctor who tells him he has Parkinson's disease – he wants to know how this could have happened to him but the doctor cannot give him an explanation – that evening, or the next, he has a dream.

He is back home in northern Ontario in a small clearing among the trees – he sees a shaman sitting beside a small fire – he is wearing a blue cloak and although surrounded by darkness the cloak shimmers like the sky on a brilliant day – he points to the fire and tells Morrisseau to look into it.

In the red embers Morrisseau sees a trapline about two hundred kilometres long – every fifty kilometres there is scaffolding with dried fish – he assumes it belongs to the Indians of the area – at the same time he realizes his Bear Spirit found the fish and ate some of it – he cannot tell when this occurred but he knows it happened quite some time ago and more than once.

He also sees the Indians got tired of having their fish stolen and decided to poison the bear and kill it – but the bear was strong – it had power – it didn't die – when he looks away from the fire the Shaman explains that Morrisseau's Bear Spirit – the bear part of him – is poisoned – in the white man's words his central nervous system is damaged.

Later he has another dream where again he finds himself staring into the shaman's fire – this time he is walking through a forest of cedar and poplar trees and sees somebody walking toward him – it is an old woman with a smiling face – in her hands she holds a tray with good things to eat like blueberries, fish and bannock – she offers the food to him and he eats.

When he has his fill, she asks, "Do you know what you just ate?"

Morrisseau looks at the tray and it is crawling with little white bugs
– they grow wings and start to buzz around him and fly off – the old
woman turns into a woodpecker and flies into one of the nearby trees –
she taps the trunk with her beak digging under the bark for bugs –
Morrisseau turns away from fire.

Again the shaman is there to interpret for him – he tells him that the
woodpecker is a good medicine woman – she gave him the plate of
insects to keep him alive – he is sick because of the poisoned fish
and she was trying to help him –she tried to dig the sickness out
of him – but there is too much of it.

This was Morrisseau's Medicine Dream

Norval Morrisseau spoke often of the importance of his grandfather Potan Nanakonagos and the teachings of Elders. Central to Ojibway epistemology is the belief in the "medicine snake," a spirit, or Manitou, that inhabits the Ojibway pantheon of Manitous, associated with shamanic power and healing.

⊕

Encircling Serpent with Ancestors, c. 1996

By now the tremors from his Parkinson's disease are beginning
to recoil through his body like gunshot, and in his confusion
he goes to a place where he can ask the necessary questions.
He is a boy again, accompanying his beloved grandfather, stopping
at a beached boat and running his hand up the smooth wood.

What catches his eye is the painted image of a horned snake
on the prow. Whoever dreams of such a snake will have the power
to become a great shaman, a conjurer who has the ability to change
the shape of things, to take kendaswin, knowledge, outside the way
of the world, all for the good of the people.

And although his grandfather is long gone, along with other elders
who have passed, old Potan explains long into the night. The artist's ears
growing like two gourd rattles keeping time to every sacred word. But
silence eventually overtakes any answer. Medicine Snake coiled and
radiant in its benevolent smile of sympathy.

Throughout his career Norval Morrisseau was surrounded by a coterie of followers,
whether they be lovers, friends, family, disciples and/or apprentices. Like a
modern-day da Vinci, Michelangelo or Raphael, with an atelier of assistants and
apprentices, the artist saw no problem working with other painters.

⊕

Apprentice, 1997

By this time it is not only the work
but about who does the work.

Who will be the next?
he announces loud and wide.

Friends, relatives, lovers, children
Lined up like colourful marbles.

Each apprentice already transformed
into a fish or a rabbit or a bird...

Enmeshed in the net of an unrelenting vision.

Invoking a theme revisited throughout his career, this painting explicitly espouses an environmental ethic. It speaks of the balance found in nature, and illustrates the intricate bond of kinship that links all life. For Morrisseau, the transformation of animals and humans indicates that the reality we know is constantly changing and not what it presumably appears to be.

⊕

Natural Balance, 1997

Examine the pretty painting:
five birds, possibly loons,
animals emerging
one out of another.
Examine the pretty colours:
rose red, apple green,
petal purple, sea blue.

Look no further
It's what you've been waiting for.
Oh, your poor confusion.

INDIAN CANOE

This work is painted on a piece of stone and executed in red paint, reminiscent of the red ochre of the original Ojibway pictographs or rock paintings, one of the earliest sources of inspiration for the artist. Marvelous in its simplicity, it speaks of continuance and the power of the imagination to inspire.

⊕

Indian Canoe, n.d.

Behind the blink of a dream
the shaman paints himself
into voyage
and travels
with the people
who have been paddling all their lives
for centuries
back to the source
of religion

Mishipesheu
water Manitou, spirit guide
swims the underworld
spiraling out of a whirlpool
Sign of medicine power
and presence
a prayer
for calm water

Loon shapes the canoe
in an elegant song
of loyalty
and beauty
head held high
to the distant horizon
vigilant for the people

Sturgeon supports
the fragile vessel
master of deep water

strength
and sweet flesh
given in self-sacrifice
beloved
totems

And the four aboard
Man, Woman, Child
Shaman (paddle or brush in hand)
painted in red ochre on stone
and bound together
transformed
innumerable times
by innumerable artists
so that the people might continue.

A Note on the Life and Art of Norval Morrisseau

Norval Morrisseau is considered by art historians, critics and curators as one of the most innovative artists of the 20th century. Among his many awards and honours are the Order of Canada and an Aboriginal Achievement Award. Referred to as the "Picasso of the North" by the French press, he was the only Canadian painter invited to France to celebrate the bi-centennial of the French Revolution in 1989. A self-taught artist, Norval Morrisseau came to the attention of the Canadian art scene in 1962 with his first solo and break-through exhibition at Pollock Gallery in Toronto. This sold-out show announced the arrival of an artist like no other in the history of Canadian art. In the first ever review of his work, *Globe and Mail* art critic Pearl McCarthy declared him a genius.

Born in 1932 in the isolated Ojibway community of Sand Point in remote northwestern Ontario, and having lived a tumultuous life of extreme highs and lows, Norval Morrisseau died in Toronto in 2007.

Drawing initially on the iconography of traditional First Nations sources, in particular the sacred birch-bark scrolls and the pictographs (or prehistoric "rock art") of the Algonquin-speaking peoples, Morrisseau would go on to incorporate a wide array of contemporary influences in his art, ranging from the techniques of modernist painters and the imagery of comic books and magazines to new-age philosophy. Continually evolving and developing as a painter, he would quickly eschew the label "primitive artist" and become renowned for his daring experiments with imagery, scale and colour, which critics would come to call no less than extraordinary and visionary. Extremely prolific, Morrisseau is credited with having executed thousands of paintings in his lifetime. Following on the heels of Morrisseau's incredible success, a younger generation of painters, both Native and non-Native, followed in his style and became known as the Woodland School of Painters, the only indigenous school of painting to emerge in Canada.

Additional information about Norval Morrisseau's art can be ob-tained from the National Gallery of Canada's website: www.gallery.ca, from private galleries and from visual arts organizations, such as www.aboriginalcuratorialcollective.org.

Acknowledgements

This book, like its companion text, the creative biography *Norval Morrisseau: Man Changing into Thunderbird,* would not exist without the input of many people. Again, I will begin by acknowledging Norval Morrisseau himself for giving me his "shamanic blessing" and challenging me "not to leave anything out," which turned into a monumental task. I suppose this is the reason for a second book. What I could not handle in prose naturally went into the poetry.

There are many people who met with me and talked openly about Norval's life, and I would like to acknowledgement them as well. Their names are in the biography. I would also like to acknowledge the numerous scholars, curators, writers, filmmakers and journalists who have written books, essays and newspaper articles and made films about Norval Morrisseau, which have been important sources of information.

I would be remiss not to give a heartfelt thanks to Harbour Publishing, and in particular Anna Comfort O'Keeffe for her continuing support, and to Nicola Goshulak who worked on the production. A Chi-Miigwetch goes out to Daniel David Moses and Rebecca Hendry for providing valuable editorial advice, and last but not least to Heather Macfarlane, my partner, for pushing me to do better. As for my use of Anishinabemowin, and any concepts associated with Ojibway intellectual traditions in the text, I take full responsibility for any errors, while acknowledging a legacy of silencing.

A Note on the Author

Armand Garnet Ruffo is a scholar and poet of Ojibway heritage. He is among the second generation of contemporary Indigenous writers in Canada to begin publishing in the late 1980s and early 1990s. His work includes *Opening in the Sky* (Theytus Books, 1994), *Grey Owl: the Mystery of Archie Belaney* (Coteau Books, 1997) and *At Geronimo's Grave* (Coteau Books, 2001). In 2001, he edited *(Ad)dressing Our Words: Aboriginal Perspectives on Aboriginal Literatures,* and, in 2013, he co-edited *An Anthology of Canadian Native Literature in English* (OUP). In 2010, his feature film, *A Windigo Tale,* won Best Picture at the 35th American Indian Film Festival in San Francisco and The Dreamspeakers Film Festival in Edmonton. Born in Chapleau, northern Ontario, he currently lives in Kingston, Ontario, Canada, and teaches at Queen's University. His poetry, fiction and non-fiction continue to be published widely.

Some of the poems have appeared in various forms in *An Anthology of Canadian Native Literature in English* (OUP), *Norval Morrisseau: Shaman Artist* (NGC), *Norval Morrisseau: Man Changing into Thunderbird* (Douglas & McIntyre), *Norval Morrisseau 2014 Retrospective* catalogue (Kinsman Robinson Galleries), *EVENT, ARC Poetry, ByWords, Ottawater, Zocalo Poets, Maple Tree Supplement, Canadian Literature, Rampike* and *Poetry Ireland Review.*